OFF THE BEATEN TRACK

A Guide to Mountain Biking in Western North Carolina

by Jim Parham

WMC Publishing, P.O. Box 158, Almond, NC 28702

Cover and Interior Design and Art by David Kareken

ISBN 0-9631861-0-8 $12.95

A great deal of information is contained in this book and every effort has been made to provide this information as accurately as possible. However, roads and trails can change with time, many roads are not marked by signs, distances may vary with individual cyclocomputers, and U.S. Forest Service rules and regulations are subject to interpretation and change. There are risks inherent in the sport of mountain biking. *The author and publisher accept no responsibility for inaccuracies or for damages incurred while attempting any of the routes listed.* **Maps in this book are not to scale.**

Printed On Recycled Paper

TABLE OF CONTENTS

Introduction

In the last several years mountain biking in western North Carolina has become more and more popular. On any given weekend during the year you can see car after car on the local highways, loaded with bikes. They come from all over the Southeast, and a good number of them come to ride on the bike trails of the Tsali Recreation Area. The others spread themselves out over the mountains, exploring even newer territories. Many of these people spend their entire vacations here. For bicycling, as well as for many other sports and recreational activities, western North Carolina rivals any region in the United States. Lakes, rivers, trails, streams, mild winters and cool summers, variety of terrain and many managed public lands make this area ideal for mountain biking. Towering above it all is the Great Smoky Mountains National Park.

Nearly all of the rugged mountain land on which the trails in this book are located lies within the Nantahala National Forest, where peaks rising to 5,000 feet and above feature the same terrain as those next door in the national park. This national forest is crisscrossed with a network of old foot trails and logging roads. Over the years most of these have been overgrown with rhododendron thickets and briar bushes. Fortunately, a number have been saved to make up the trails we see on the topographic maps of today. Many are perfect for mountain biking.

Along with the trails is a scattering of gated forest service gravel roads, originally constructed to open up tracts of land for timber harvesting. These roads have become biking highways into what was once remote territory. They'll take you to the highest ridges with views of majestic mountains, green valleys, rivers and lakes. On some rides the configuration of a paved road or old trail may curve around to form a perfect loop. On others, you pedal out to the end of a long uphill, then just turn around and go for a screaming ride back down the mountain.

Locally, there's a small group of bikers who are constantly on the lookout for new and different riding trails. For this crowd, a jovial call on the phone one evening may mean the next day will be spent riding the "best trail ever," or more often than not lost on some remote, long-forgotten track, cold and hungry. It's from exploratory rides such as these that many of the trails in this book were discovered. Only after many miles of pedaling and many more wrong turns were they fine-tuned, measured, and mapped.

I think you'll enjoy exploring the 25 trails listed in this book. Any one of them can easily be done in a day, most in an afternoon. If you're heading out for the first time, you may want to explore the shorter rides with less climbing at first, while building yourself up for the longer and more difficult rides. If you're an expert, don't worry—there is plenty here to challenge your skills. No matter what your ability level, you'll find this area hard to beat for mountain biking.

The Trails

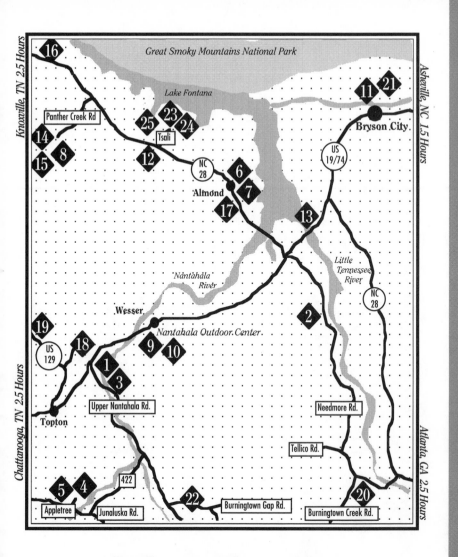

Great Smoky Mountains National Park

Lake Fontana

Panther Creek Rd

Tsali

Bryson City

US
19/74

NC
28

Almond

Little
Tennessee
River

NC
28

Nantahala
River

Wesser

Nantahala Outdoor Center

US
129

Upper Nantahala Rd.

Needmore Rd.

Topton

Tellico Rd.

422

Appletree

Junaluska Rd.

Burningtown Gap Rd.

Burningtown Creek Rd.

Orientation Map

COMBINA- TION RIDES

1– Winding Stairs • 13.7 Miles
2– Swinging Bridge • 11.6 Miles
3– Upper Nantahala • 18.6 Miles
4– Diamond Valley • 8.7 Miles
5– London Bald • 12.6 Miles
6– Turkey Branch • 8.3 Miles
7– Grapevine Cove • 7 Miles
8– Shell Stand Creek • 6.3 Miles
9– Wesser Bald • 28.3 Miles
10– Tellico Gap • 24.4 Miles
11– Cowee Bald • 35 Miles

Winding Stairs

This is a wonderful ride. The first 5 miles are almost entirely uphill, ending up beside a beautiful lake. The last half is a great downhill coast alongside the cascades of the upper Nantahala River.

Start/Finish

Public Launch site for Nantahala River on US 19/74

Trail Configuration

Loop

Surface

Pavement • 8.4 miles
Gravel road • 5.3 miles

Highlights

Whitewater rafting, views of Nantahala Gorge, long uphill, Queen's Lake (great for swimming after long hill climb), long downhill, cascades and waterfalls

Total Distance

13.7 miles

Time Allowance

Beginner • 2.5 hours
Intermediate • 1.75 hours
Advanced • 1.25 hours

Mileposts

- From start, turn right (east) on US 19/74.
- Mile 1.1-- turn right onto Winding Stairs Road (Forest Service Road 422).
- Mile 4.4-- this is the top of the hill and Queen's Lake will be on the right.
- Mile 5.5-- take left fork.
- Mile 6.4-- gravel ends and pavement begins.
- Mile 9.2-- turn right at stop sign by Nantahala School. This is the Upper Nantahala road.
- Mile 13.7-- finish.

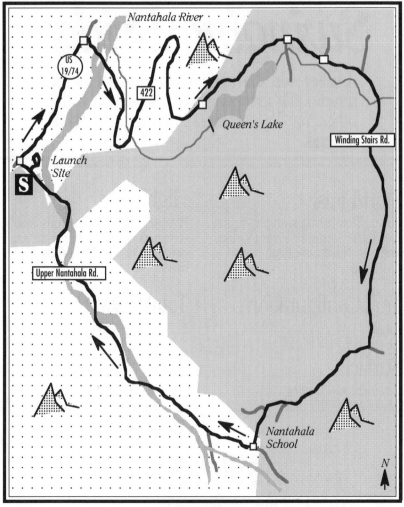

Nantahala River

US 19/74

422

Queen's Lake

Winding Stairs Rd.

Launch Site

S

Upper Nantahala Rd.

Nantahala School

N

MAP KEY

Bike Trail..........................	⌇	Forest Service Rd. #.................	419
Other Trail or Road..........	⌇	County Road Name............	Watia Rd.
Direction of Travel...............	➤	Foot Trail.........................	~~~~~
Start/Finish..........................	S	Timber Cut.....................	▨
Milepost..............................	□		
Public Land......................	⬚		
Private Land.....................	▦		
Railroad Tracks..............	┼┼┼		
Major Mountain..................	⛰		
River, Lake, or Stream.....	∿		

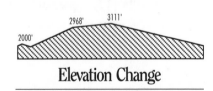

2000'   2968'   3111'

Elevation Change

Swinging Bridge

A valley ride, this one goes up one side of the serene Little Tennessee River and back down the other. You'll pedal across a swinging bridge at the end.

Start/Finish

Dirt pull-off beside swinging bridge over Little Tennesee River (4 miles south on Needmore Road from US 19/74)

Highlights

Mountain views, some hills, one screamer downhill, blind curves, swinging bridge, Little Tennessee River

Trail Configuration

Loop

Total Distance

11.6 miles

Surface

Pavement • 6.7 miles
Gravel road • 4.9 miles

Time Allowance

Beginner • 2 hours
Intermediate • 1.5 hours
Advanced • 1 hour

Mileposts

- From start, turn left onto Needmore Road.
- Mile 1.7-- road turns to dirt, continue straight.
- Mile 5-- gravel road ends, turn left onto Tellico Road.
- Mile 5.3-- road forks, take left fork.
- Mile 6.2-- road turns left and crosses river. Cross bridge and turn left onto NC 28.
- Mile 10-- turn left onto dirt road. It's marked by a sign for Brush Creek Baptist Church.
- Mile 11.6-- cross swinging bridge to finish.

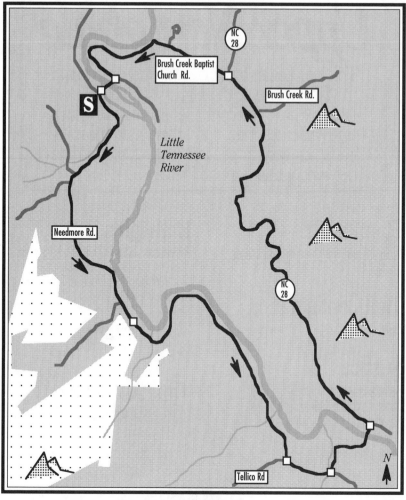

Little Tennessee River

Brush Creek Baptist Church Rd.

NC 28

Brush Creek Rd.

Needmore Rd.

NC 28

Tellico Rd

N

MAP KEY

Bike Trail..........................

Other Trail or Road...........

Direction of Travel...............

Start/Finish............................. S

Milepost................................... □

Public Land.......................

Private Land......................

Railroad Tracks...............

Major Mountain...................

River, Lake, or Stream.....

Forest Service Rd. #................. 419

County Road Name............. Watia Rd.

Foot Trail.........................

Timber Cut.....................

1800'   2280'   2200'

Elevation Change

Upper Nantahala

This loop begins by winding its way up through the far reaches of the Upper Nantahala River drainage area, and combines paved roads with a true wilderness ride. Pay attention to the mileposts; it's easy to get lost while exploring the network of trails around Pierce Creek.

Start/Finish

Launch site for Nantahala River on US 19/74

Trail Configuration

Loop

Surface

Single track • 9.5 miles
Gravel road • 3.9 miles
Pavement • 5.2 miles

Highlights

River cascades, Nantahala power project pipeline, hidden trails, thick rhododendron and conifer forest, views, rocky surface

Total Distance

18.6 miles

Time Allowance

Beginner • 5.5 hours
Intermediate • 4 hours
Advanced • 2.5 hours

Mileposts

- From start, turn left out of Nantahala launch area onto Upper Nantahala road.
- Mile 4.1-- turn right onto 308 (gravel). Continue following river.
- Mile 7.5-- turn right onto Junaluska Rd., cross river, then take immediate right through gate into Appletree Group Campground.
- Mile 7.7-- take right fork on 7208, continue past campground and through gate up reclaimed road bed.
- Mile 11.4-- turn right onto hiker trail. 100 yards onto this trail two old roadbeds turn off to the right--**stay left** both times.
- Mile 14.1-- double creek crossing, then turn left onto Nantahala River trail (blue blazes).
- Mile 14.2-- Laurel Creek trail turns off to left (orange blaze), **continue up Nantahala River trail** (blue blazes).

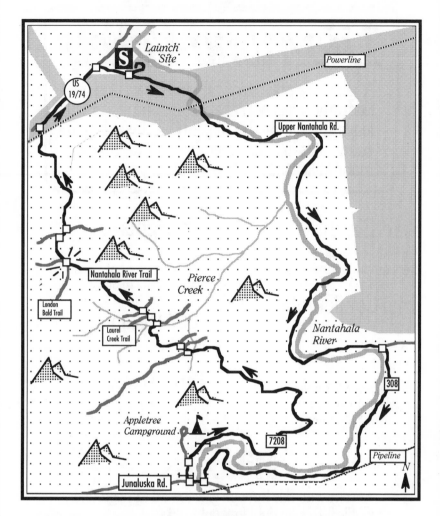

- Mile 14.3-- trail has a fork to the left and then one to the right. Stay on middle trail and continue to follow blue blazes up hill.
- Mile 15.7-- jct. with London Bald trail which turns back to the left. The N. R. trail ends here as two trails split off in front. One continues uphill to the left while the other turns downhill to the right. Take the right fork downhill.
- Mile 16.1-- a trail enters from the left, go straight 20 yds. and then turn left at the next trail junction.
- Mile 17.5-- ride out driveway to Hwy. 19/74 and turn right.
- Mile 18.6-- finish.

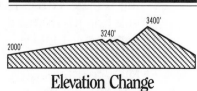

Elevation Change

Diamond Valley

A gem of a ride. This trail winds its way up one side of the upper Nantahala Gorge on a reclaimed logging road for the majority of the ride and culminates in a screamer downhill on the Diamond Valley trail back to the start.

Start/Finish

Entrance to Appletree Group Campground on Junaluska Road

Trail Configuration

Loop

Surface

Single track • 7.1 miles
Gravel road • 0.4 miles
Pavement • 1.2 miles

Highlights

Beautiful campground, bogs, loose rock, steep descent, deadfalls, views, creek crossings

Total Distance

8.7 miles

Time Allowance

Beginner • 3 hours
Intermediate • 2 hours
Advanced • 1 hour

Mileposts

- From start, ride through gate toward campground.
- Mile 0.1-- take right fork onto 7208.
- Mile 0.4-- go through gate and up reclaimed logging road.
- Mile 3.9-- hiker trail sign on right, stay on reclaimed logging road.
- Mile 4.9-- road forks. Stay on right fork.
- Mile 6-- hiker trail sign on left. Take this trail. Ride approximately 50 yds. and a trail marked with yellow blazes crosses road bed. Turn right.
- Mile 6.3-- jct. Diamond Valley trail on edge of timber cut. Turn left (white blazes).
- Mile 7.4-- cross Junaluska Trail.
- Mile 7.5-- jct. Junaluska Rd. Turn left.
- Mile 8.7-- finish.

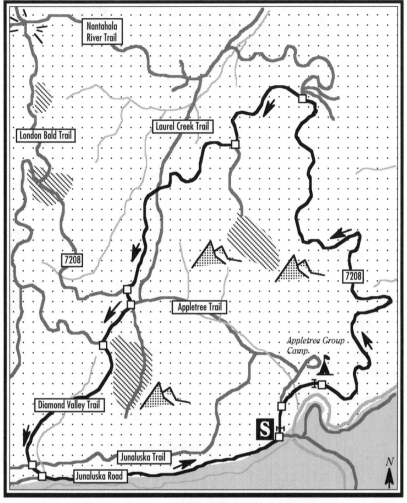

Nantahala River Trail

London Bald Trail

Laurel Creek Trail

7208

7208

Appletree Trail

Appletree Group Camp.

Diamond Valley Trail

Junaluska Trail

Junaluska Road

S

N

MAP KEY

Bike Trail............................

Other Trail or Road...........

Direction of Travel............... →

Start/Finish........................ **S**

Milepost............................. □

Public Land.......................

Private Land.....................

Railroad Tracks.............. ┼┼┼

Major Mountain..................

River, Lake, or Stream.....

Forest Service Rd. #.................. 419

County Road Name............. Watia Rd.

Foot Trail........................

Timber Cut......................

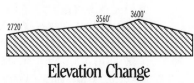

2720'   3560'   3600'

Elevation Change

London Bald

Almost entirely single track, this ride packs a lot of punch. Some of the steep grades may require walking. This trail needs to be ridden or parts of it will be lost to the underbrush.

Start/Finish

Entrance to Appletree Group Campground on Junaluska Road

Trail Configuration

Loop

Surface

Single track • 11 miles
Gravel road • 0.4 miles
Pavement • 1.2 miles

Highlights

Long climbs, deadfalls, creek crossings, loose rocks, good views, timber cuts, steep grades, whoop-te-doos, gripper downhill

Total Distance

12.6 miles

Time Allowance

Beginner • 5.5 hours
Intermediate • 4 hours
Advanced • 2.5 hours

Mileposts

- From start, ride through entrance gate to Appletree.
- Mile 0.1-- take right fork onto 7208.
- Mile 0.4-- go through gate and up reclaimed road.
- Mile 3.9-- turn right onto hiker trail. 100 yds. into woods 2 trails fork to right; stay left both times.
- Mile 4.8-- ride through clearing in wood (white blazes).
- Mile 5.2-- double creek crossing, then turn left onto Nantahala River trail (blue blazes).
- Mile 5.3-- Laurel Creek trail turns off to left; stay right (blue blazes) on Nantahala River trail.
- Mile 5.4-- a trail forks off to the left and a little beyond another forks off to the right. Stay on center trail (blue blazes).

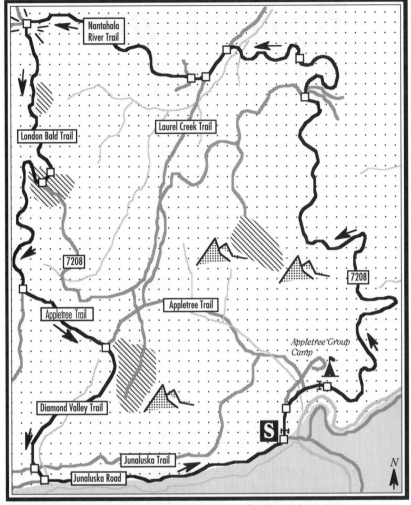

- Mile 6.6– jct. London Bald trail. Turn left (blue blazes).
- Mile 8.2– trail enters timber cut.
- Mile 8.4– hiker trail sign. Turn sharply to right and follow blue blazes up the hill.
- Mile 9.4– jct. Appletree trail. Turn left down steep hill (yellow blazes).
- Mile 10.2– jct. Diamond Valley trail at edge of timber cut. Turn right onto D.V. trail (white blazes).
- Mile 11.3– cross Junaluska trail.
- Mile 11.4– turn left on Junaluska Road.
- Mile 12.6– finish.

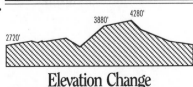

Elevation Change

Turkey Branch

A great afternoon hill workout, this trail climbs steeply up a ridge on an old road and then loops around on a gated forest service road and back down NC 28 to the start.

Start/Finish

Almond Post Office on NC 28

Trail Configuration

Loop

Surface

Single track • 1.4 miles
Gravel road • 4.9 miles
Pavement • 2 miles

Highlights

Views of Great Smokies National Park, long steep uphill, long downhill

Total Distance

8.3 miles

Time Allowance

Beginner • 2 hours
Intermediate • 1.5 hours
Advanced • 1 hour

Mileposts

- From start, take Turkey Branch road (directly across from Post Office--it looks like a driveway).
- Mile 1-- road forks; take left fork which goes through open gate.
- Mile 1.4-- road crossing; continue straight.
- Mile 1.7-- road forks; take right fork.
- Mile 2.4-- road dead-ends into 2630; turn right.
- Mile 4.6-- dead-end road enters from left.
- Mile 6.3-- junction NC 28; turn right.
- Mile 8.3-- finish.

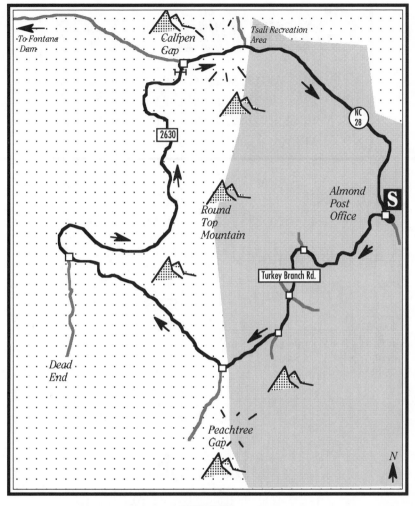

MAP KEY

Bike Trail.......................
Other Trail or Road...........
Direction of Travel............... →
Start/Finish........................... **S**
Milepost.................................. □
Public Land.......................
Private Land......................
Railroad Tracks.............. —+—+—+—
Major Mountain..................
River, Lake, or Stream.....

Forest Service Rd. #................. 419
County Road Name............. Watia Rd.
Foot Trail........................ ∿∿∿∿∿∿
Timber Cut......................

Elevation Change

Grapevine Cove

Beginning with a steep climb, followed by 1.3 miles of very technical riding, this ride will really test your skills, *and* there are more whoop-te-doos than you'll care to count.

Start/Finish
Almond Post Office on NC 28

Trail Configuration
Loop

Surface
Single track • 2.7 miles
Gravel road • 3.5 miles
Pavement • 0.8 miles

Highlights
Slick rocks, numerous creek crossings, whoop-te-doos, loose rocks, nice views of Lake Fontana and Smokies

Total Distance
7 miles

Time Allowance
Beginner • 2.5 hours
Intermediate • 2 hours
Advanced • 1.25 hours

Mileposts

- From start, ride up Turkey Branch road (directly across highway from Post Office-it looks like a driveway).
- Mile 1-- road forks; turn back to left through open gate.
- Mile 1.4-- top of hill and road splits three ways; take far left road and head for whoop-te-doos on Grapevine Cove trail.
- Mile 2.7-- jct. Watia Road; turn left.
- Mile 6.2-- turn left onto NC 28.
- Mile 7-- finish.

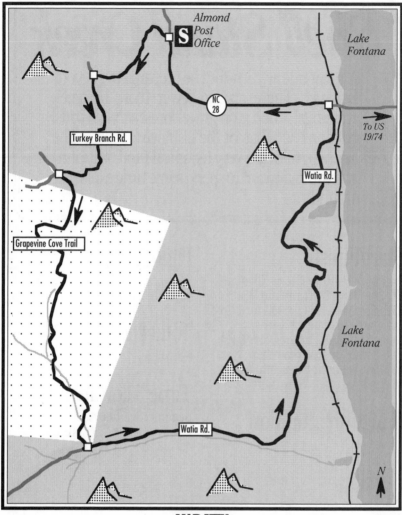

MAP KEY

Bike Trail.......................

Other Trail or Road...........

Direction of Travel............... →

Start/Finish....................... **S**

Milepost................................. □

Public Land...................... · · · ·

Private Land....................

Railroad Tracks............... ┼┼┼┼

Major Mountain................

River, Lake, or Stream.....

Forest Service Rd. #................. 419

County Road Name............. Watia Rd.

Foot Trail........................

Timber Cut......................

Elevation Change

1860'   2580'   1920'

19

Shell Stand Creek

A great ride anytime but be prepared to get your feet wet. There are no fewer than 14 creek crossings! Much is on gravel forest service roads, but don't let that or the distance fool you. The last two miles are very technical (and beautiful) and you may want to spend some time exploring around.

Start/Finish

On upper Panther Creek Rd. off of NC 28. Drive to Tumbling Waters Campground and take left fork up the gravel road which is the continuation of Panther Creek Rd. Half a mile up this road there is a pull-out before it turns into a four wheel drive road. Start here.

Trail Configuration

Loop

Surface

Gravel road • 4.2 miles
Single track • 2.1 miles

Highlights

Spectacular views, creek crossings, sheer road cuts, timber cuts

Total Distance

6.3 miles

Time Allowance

Beginner • 3 hours
Intermediate • 2.5 hours
Advanced • 1.75 hours

Mileposts

- From start, ride back toward campground.
- Mile 0.5-- turn left onto Shell Stand Road (418).
- Mile 2.8-- turn left through gate onto 419.
- Mile 4.2-turn left after crossing creek onto single track (4WD road).
- Mile 5-- this is the last of several meadows and it seems that the road ends here. Don't give up the search! You'll find it continues at the far end of the meadow and follows the creek.
- Mile 6-- take left fork still heading downstream.
- Mile 6.2-- go through gate and take left fork.
- Mile 6.3-- finish.

Bulletin

April 20, 1992

After this book was published, the author was notified that by order of the Forest Supervisor in North Carolina, "driving, riding, possessing, parking or leaving any kind of transportation on a developed trail not designated, and so posted for that specific use" is prohibited. This means that mountain bikes are allowed only on trails signed for their use and any unsigned, developed trail should be considered closed to bikes. Bikes are allowed on gated and closed Forest Service roads. This is the policy, although Forest Service maps, brochures, and some signs do not yet reflect it.

The Forest Service pursues an ongoing program of assessing its trail system for use by mountain bikes. Current trail designations are subject to change. Portions of the Diamond Valley route (mile 6 to mile 7.5), the London Bald route (mile 3.9 to mile 11.4), the Upper Nantahala route (mile 11.4 to mile 15.7), the Wesser Bald route (mile 22.4 to mile 25.7), and the Tellico Gap route (mile 18.5 to mile 21.8) follow trails that at this date are closed to bikes.

In addition, sections of the Wesser Bald route (mile 21.7 to mile 22.4), and the Tellico Gap route (mile 17.8 to mile 18.5) follow the Appalachian National Scenic Trail. Forest Service regulations prohibit possessing, carrying, pushing or parking a bicycle on this trail. This regulation is not subject to change.

For up-to-date trail information, to volunteer a group for trail building or maintenance, to inquire about scouting new routes, or to make suggestions for future mountain biking opportunities contact:

Wayah Ranger District
8 Sloan Road
Franklin, NC 28734
704/524-6441

Cheoah Ranger District
Route 1, Box 16-A
Robbinsville, NC 28771
704/479-6431

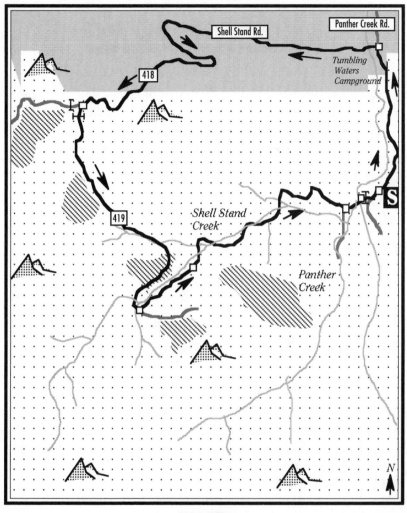

MAP KEY

Bike Trail............................	Forest Service Rd. #................. 419
Other Trail or Road...........	County Road Name............. Watia Rd.
Direction of Travel...............	Foot Trail........................
Start/Finish.................... S	Timber Cut.....................
Milepost.......................... □	
Public Land.....................	
Private Land....................	
Railroad Tracks..............	
Major Mountain..................	
River, Lake, or Stream.....	

Elevation Change

1960' 2760' 2600'

Wesser Bald

This is a long ride that takes you through all the best that western North Carolina has to offer. A beautiful river, green valleys, and a long climb to a lookout tower make this an unforgettable ride.

Start/Finish

Nantahala Outdoor Center (NOC) on US 19/74

Trail Configuration

Loop

Surface

Single track • 4.9 miles
Gravel road • 9.1 miles
Pavement • 14.3 miles

Highlights

Little Tennessee River, very steep climb, lookout tower, technical single track and spectacular views

Total Distance

28.3 miles

Time Allowance

Beginner • 6.5 hours
Intermediate • 5 hours
Advanced • 3.75 hours

Mileposts

- From start, ride east on US 19/74.
- Mile 4.5– jct. of NC 28, US 19/74, and Needmore Road. Turn right onto Needmore Rd.
- Mile 10.3– pavement ends.
- Mile 13.6– gravel road ends; turn right on Tellico Road.
- Mile 15.5– pavement ends.
- Mile 15.7– road forks; take right fork (follow sign to Tellico Trout).
- Mile 16.4– Tellico Trout Farm.
- Mile 16.9– road forks. Take right fork in front of white house.
- Mile 20.8– Tellico Gap. Turn right and continue up hill on 4 wheel drive road (it is very steep for next mile up to tower).
- Mile 21.7– top of Wesser Bald. *Carry bike on Appalachian Trail.*
- Mile 22.3– trail to spring marked by blue blazes. Continue straight.
- Mile 22.4– turn right onto Wesser Creek trail (dark blue blazes).
- Mile 25.7– trail becomes gravel road (after many switch backs).
- Mile 26.2– pavement begins.
- Mile 27.4– turn left onto US 19/74.
- Mile 28.3– finish.

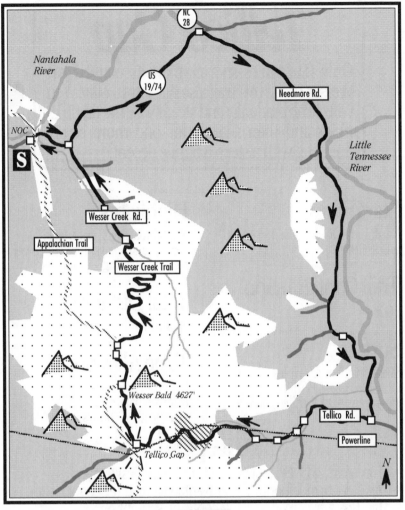

Nantahala
River

NC
28

US
19/74

Needmore Rd.

NOC

S

Little
Tennessee
River

Wesser Creek Rd.

Appalachian Trail

Wesser Creek Trail

Wesser Bald 4627'

Tellico Rd.

Powerline

Tellico Gap

N

MAP KEY

Bike Trail............................	～
Other Trail or Road...........	～
Direction of Travel..............	➤
Start/Finish.........................	**S**
Milepost..............................	□
Public Land.........................	
Private Land........................	
Railroad Tracks..................	＋＋＋
Major Mountain...................	⛰
River, Lake, or Stream......	～

Forest Service Rd. #..................	419
County Road Name.............	Watia Rd.
Foot Trail..........................	﹀﹀﹀
Timber Cut........................	▨

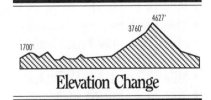

1700'   3760'   4627'

Elevation Change

23

Tellico Gap

Only four miles shorter than its counterpart Wesser Bald, this trail also has lots to offer. You will climb gradually and steadily for the first 16.9 miles and then sharply for one more before finishing with a steep 6.5 mile decent.

Start/Finish

Nantahala Outdoor Center (NOC) on US 19/74

Trail Configuration

Loop

Surface

Single track • 4.9 miles
Gravel road • 4.6 miles
Pavement • 14.9 miles

Highlights

Nantahala River,waterfalls, spectacular views, lookout tower, technical riding

Total Distance

24.4 miles

Time Allowance

Beginner • 6 hours
Intermediate • 4.5 hours
Advanced • 3 hours

Mileposts

- From start, go west on US 19/74 upstream beside river.
- Mile 7.8-- turn left onto Upper Nantahala road (at Launch site).
- Mile 12-- gravel road to right; continue straight on.
- Mile 12.3-- road to Nantahala School on left; continue straight on.
- Mile 12.8-- turn left on Tellico Gap Rd. (follow sign to Tellico Gap); road turns to gravel.
- Mile 14.6-- road enters from left; continue straight on.
- Mile 15.4-- road forks; take right fork.
- Mile 16.9-- Tellico Gap; turn left and continue up 4WD road.
- Mile 17.8-- Wesser Bald lookout tower. *Carry bike on AT.*
- Mile 18.4-- blue blazes mark trail to spring.
- Mile 18.5-- turn right onto Wesser Creek Trail (blue blazes).
- Mile 21.8-- gravel road begins.
- Mile 22.3-- pavement begins.
- Mile 23.5-- jct. US 19/74; turn left.
- Mile 24.4-- finish.

NOTE: 7/10 of a mile on this loop follows the Appalachian Trail. Please respect the AT and carry your bike.

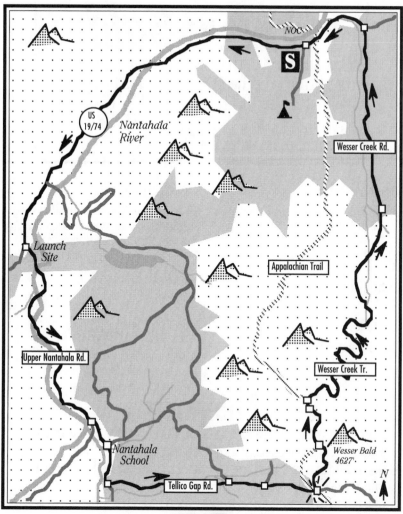

MAP KEY

Bike Trail......................	Forest Service Rd. #................. 419
Other Trail or Road...........	County Road Name............ Watia Rd.
Direction of Travel.............. →	Foot Trail.......................
Start/Finish........................... S	Timber Cut.................
Milepost.................................. □	
Public Land......................	
Private Land....................	
Railroad Tracks..............	
Major Mountain.................	
River, Lake, or Stream.....	

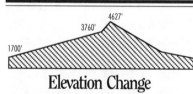

1700' 3760' 4627'

Elevation Change

Cowee Bald

This ride is both strenuous and beautiful. You'll travel from the heart of Bryson City up to a lookout tower from which Sylva, Cherokee, Bryson City, and Franklin all are visible. 17 downhill miles later you'll be back in Bryson.

Start/Finish

Great Smoky Mountain Railway depot in Bryson City

Trail Configuration

Loop with extension

Surface

Gravel road • 15 miles
Pavement • 20 miles

Highlights

Long uphills and downhills, steep grades, spectacular views, creek crossings, beautiful valleys

Total Distance

35 miles

Time Allowance

Beginner • 7 hours
Intermediate • 5 hours
Advanced • 3.5 hours

Mileposts

- From start, ride toward Carolina Building Supply. Cross tracks and follow signs for Recreation Department.
- Mile 0.1-- turn left on Ramseur Street, then immediately right onto Deep Creek Rd.
- Mile 0.6-- turn right, cross bridge, then cross to right side of tracks and follow gravel road along Tuckaseegee River.
- Mile 2-- turn right onto US 19, cross river, and take immediate left up beside river.
- Mile 3.6-- intersection of road that leads to four-lane; continue straight across.
- Mile 4.4-- turn right, cross over four lane and then turn left.
- Mile 5-- pavement ends.
- Mile 5.6-- pavement begins again.
- Mile 6.1-- turn right up Connelly Creek Road. Several roads will turn off to the right as you ride up the valley; always bear left.
- Mile 10.6-- pavement ends.
- Mile 14.4-- top of Wesser Gap; road branches in four different directions. Go straight (second road from right) on the road with the Alarka Laurel sign.

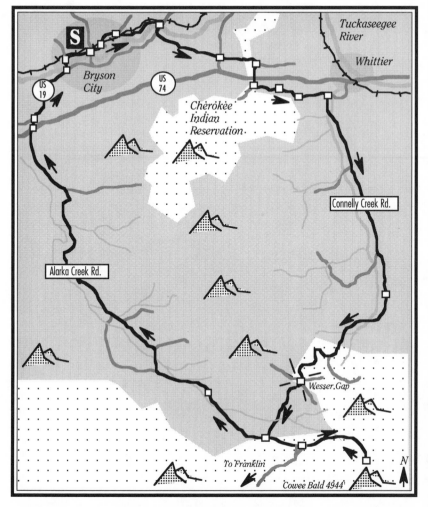

- Mile 15.4-- road forks. Turn left to Cowee Lookout Tower (right fork is the way down Alarka Creek and back to Bryson).
- Mile 15.8-- road splits, turn left uphill (a right turn here would take you to Franklin).
- Mile 17.8-- Cowee Bald Lookout tower; turn around here.
- Mile 19.8-- take right fork.
- Mile 20.2-- turn sharply back to left (right goes back to Wesser Gap). This is Alarka Creek Road.
- Mile 22.7-- road turns to pavement.
- Mile 31.5-- cross four-lane.
- Mile 31.6-- turn right and follow US 19 into Bryson.
- Mile 35-- finish.

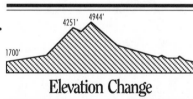

Elevation Change

GATED FOREST SERVICE ROADS

12– Calfpen Gap • 13.4 Miles
13– Old 19 Discovery • 6 Miles
14– Shell Stand Left Fork • 15.8 Miles
15– Shell Stand Right Fork • 18.2 Miles
16– Meetinghouse • 16 Miles
17– Watia Road • 15.4 Miles
18– Cheoah Bald • 15 Miles
19– Juts Gap • 10 Miles

Calfpen Gap

Just across from Tsali, this ride follows the county line southwest as it climbs the ridge from the gap. Landslides, plus some tall grass, make getting to the end of this one a little difficult. Turn around if it gets too tough; the downhill is great!

Start/Finish

Entrance to Tsali Recreation Area on NC 28

Trail Configuration

Out-and-Back

Surface

Gravel road • 12.8 miles
Pavement • 0.6 miles

Highlights

Views of Great Smokies National Park, steep dropoffs beside trail

Total Distance

13.4 miles

Time Allowance

Beginner • 3 hours
Intermediate • 2 hours
Advanced • 1.25 hours

Mileposts

- From start, turn right on NC 28.
- Mile 0.3-- turn left onto 2630.
- Mile 2-- road forks, take left fork.
- Mile 6.7-- road dead-ends, turn around.
- Mile 13.4-- finish.

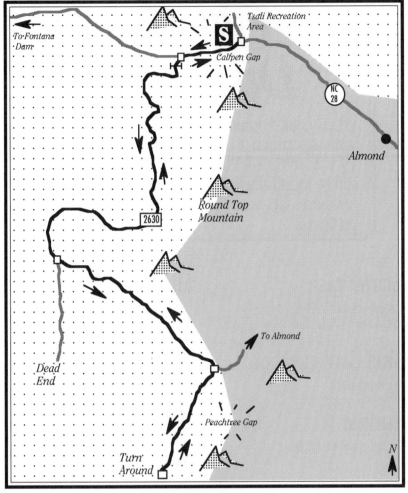

MAP KEY

Bike Trail............................
Other Trail or Road...........
Direction of Travel............... →
Start/Finish........................... **S**
Milepost............................. □
Public Land......................
Private Land.....................
Railroad Tracks.............. ┼┼┼┼
Major Mountain..................
River, Lake, or Stream.....

Forest Service Rd. #................. 419
County Road Name............. Watia Rd.
Foot Trail.............................
Timber Cut......................

Elevation Change

2200'   2800'

Old 19 Discovery

When Lake Fontana flooded the valleys many years ago, much of the road was covered and US 19 was rerouted. Parts of the old highway can still be found starting from nowhere and going nowhere. Get ready for a rollercoaster ride to get there!

Start/Finish

Captain Sandlin Bridge on US 19/74 over Little Tennessee River

Trail Configuration

Out-and-Back

Surface

Gravel road • 6 miles

Highlights

Old overgrown highway, panoramic views, Lake Fontana, superb riding surface

Total Distance

6 miles

Time Allowance

Beginner • 3 hours
Intermediate • 2 hours
Advanced • 1 hour

Mileposts

- From start, ride down asphalt road (7013) toward lake; it turns to gravel in about 100 yards.
- Mile 0.1-- take left fork up gated road. (7013)
- Mile 1.9-- take left fork; stay on main road.
- Mile 2.4-- take left fork at top of knoll.
- Mile 2.5-- turn left on concrete (this is old 19), and you will dead-end into lake at 3 mile mark. Turn right on concrete and you will dead-end at railroad tracks at 3 mile mark. Turn around.
- Mile 6-- finish.

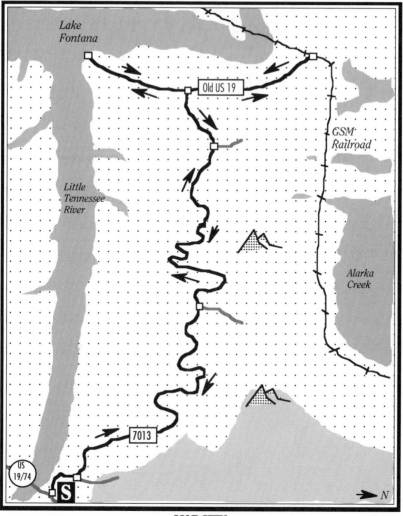

Lake
Fontana

Old US 19

GSM
Railroad

Little
Tennessee
River

Alarka
Creek

7013

US
19/74

S

N

MAP KEY

Bike Trail........................	⌇	Forest Service Rd. #..................	419
Other Trail or Road...........	⌇	County Road Name..............	Watia Rd.
Direction of Travel..............	→	Foot Trail.......................	⌇⌇⌇⌇⌇
Start/Finish....................	**S**	Timber Cut.....................	▨
Milepost.......................	□		
Public Land.....................	⸭		
Private Land....................	▨		
Railroad Tracks..............	┼┼┼		
Major Mountain.................	⛰		
River, Lake, or Stream.....	⌇		

1800'   2200'
              1720'

Elevation Change

14

Shell Stand Left Fork

This forest service road winds its way through the inner and lower elevations of Shell Stand Cove, a remote drainage that feeds Panther Creek and Lake Fontana.

Start/Finish

Off NC 28, turn onto Panther Creek Road. At campground, turn right and park on grass road shoulder. Start here.

Trail Configuration

Out-and-Back

Surface

Gravel road • 15.8 miles

Highlights

Views of Smokies, loose gravel, timber cuts, long hills

Total Distance

15.8 miles

Time Allowance

Beginner • 3 hours
Intermediate • 2 hours
Advanced • 1 hour

Mileposts

- From start, ride out Shell Stand Road.
- Mile 1.2-- road turns into Forest Service Road 418.
- Mile 2.5-- road forks with a gate at each fork; take left fork (Forest Service Road 419).
- Mile 7.9-- road dead-ends; turn around here.
- Mile 15.8-- finish.

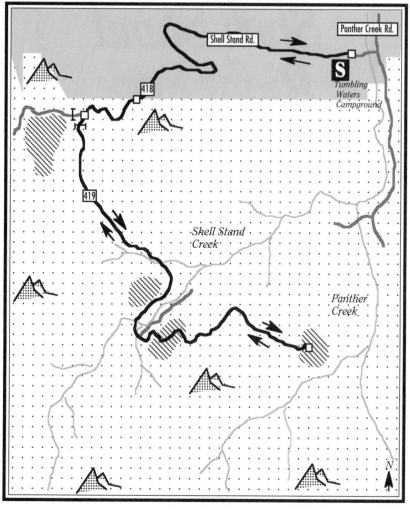

MAP KEY

Bike Trail.............................. 〜

Other Trail or Road........... 〜

Direction of Travel............... ➔

Start/Finish.......................... **S**

Milepost.................................. □

Public Land...................... ▭

Private Land..................... ▬

Railroad Tracks.............. ┼┼┼

Major Mountain................... ⛰

River, Lake, or Stream..... 〜

Forest Service Rd. #................. 419

County Road Name............. Watia Rd.

Foot Trail........................ 〜〜〜

Timber Cut...................... ▨

Elevation Change

1880' 2760' 2800'

15

Shell Stand Right Fork

This road follows the outer edges of Shell Stand Cove, ending high above the valley overlooking the Smokies. Keep an eye out for wild turkey!

Start/Finish

Off NC 28, turn onto Panther Creek Road. At campground, turn right and park on grass road shoulder. Start here.

Trail Configuration

Out-and-Back

Surface

Gravel road • 18.2 miles

Highlights

Great views of Smokies, good riding surface, some loose gravel, long hills, timber cuts

Total Distance

18.2 miles

Time Allowance

Beginner • 3.5 hours
Intermediate • 2.5 hours
Advanced • 1.75 hours

Mileposts

- From start, ride out Shell Stand Road.
- Mile 1.2-- road turns into Forest Service Road 418.
- Mile 2.5-- road forks with a gate on each fork; take right fork.
- Mile 9.1-- road dead-ends; turn around here.
- Mile 18.2-- finish.

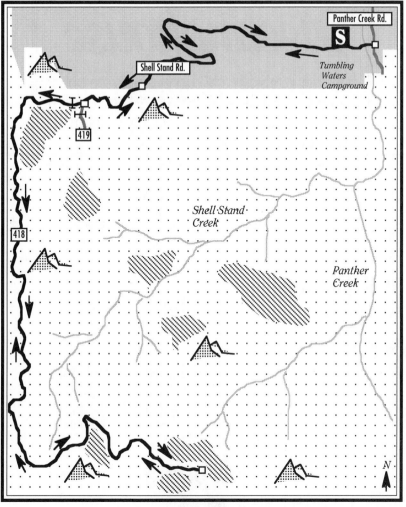

MAP KEY

Bike Trail............................ ⌇

Other Trail or Road........... ⌇

Direction of Travel............... →

Start/Finish........................... **S**

Milepost.................................... ☐

Public Land........................ ⦂⦂⦂

Private Land......................

Railroad Tracks............... ┼┼┼

Major Mountain................... ⛰

River, Lake, or Stream..... ⌇

Forest Service Rd. #................. 419

County Road Name............. Watia Rd.

Foot Trail........................ ⌇⌇⌇⌇⌇

Timber Cut...................... ▨

Elevation Change

1880' 3120' 3440'

16

Meetinghouse

This ride is so twisty and curvy you can see where you are going long before you get there. With numerous side roads there's plenty of room for exploring on this one.

Start/Finish

At gate to Forest Service Road 2540, 3.5 miles west of Tsali on NC 28

Trail Configuration

Out-and-Back

Surface

Gravel road • 16 miles

Highlights

Panoramic views of Smokies and Lake Fontana, gravel, logging operations, fast downhills, long gradual uphills

Total Distance

16 miles

Time Allowance

Beginner • 3 hours
Intermediate • 2.25 hours
Advanced • 1.75 hours

Mileposts

- From start, ride through gate and up hill. Numerous small logging roads will branch off; stay on main road.
- Mile 8-- turn around and return same way.
- Mile 16-- finish.

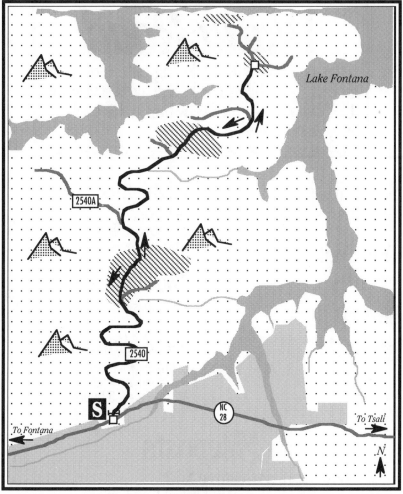

MAP KEY

Bike Trail............................ 〰

Other Trail or Road........... 〰

Direction of Travel............... →

Start/Finish............................ **S**

Milepost................................ □

Public Land....................... ⬚

Private Land...................... ▨

Railroad Tracks.............. ┼┼┼

Major Mountain................... ⛰

River, Lake, or Stream..... 〰

Forest Service Rd. #................. 419

County Road Name............. Watia Rd.

Foot Trail......................... 〰

Timber Cut..................... ▨

1800'   2000'

Elevation Change

17

Watia Road

Characterized by long sloping hills, mountain homes, a babbling creek, and the best view up the Nantahala Gorge of any trail in this book. A very enjoyable ride.

Start/Finish

Almond Post Office on NC 28

Trail Configuration

Out-and-Back

Surface

Gravel road • 13.8 miles
Pavement • 1.6 miles

Highlights

Hills, barking dogs, scenic views, cool stream, Appalachian Trail crossing, loose gravel

Total Distance

15.4 miles

Time Allowance

Beginner • 3.5 hours
Intermediate • 2.5 hours
Advanced • 1.5 hours

Mileposts

- From start, ride south on NC 28.
- Mile 0.8-- turn right just before Lake Fontana bridge onto Watia Road.
- Mile 6.5-- take right fork through gate and up Forest Service road.
- Mile 7.7-- road dead-ends; turn around and go back the way you came.
- Mile 15.4-- finish.

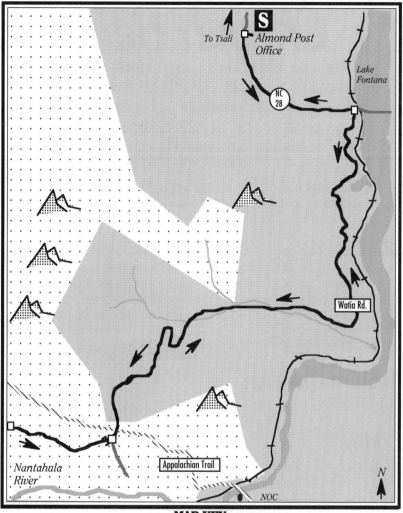

To Tsali

S

Almond Post
Office

Lake
Fontana

NC
28

Watia Rd.

Nantahala
River

Appalachian Trail

NOC

N

MAP KEY

Bike Trail............................	Forest Service Rd. #................. `419`
Other Trail or Road...........	County Road Name............. `Watia Rd.`
Direction of Travel............... →	Foot Trail.......................
Start/Finish............................ **S**	Timber Cut.....................
Milepost................................... □	
Public Land.......................	
Private Land.....................	
Railroad Tracks.............. ┼┼┼	
Major Mountain..................	
River, Lake, or Stream.....	

1860'   2400'   2300'

Elevation Change

18

Cheoah Bald

This ride takes you to the highest elevation reachable by bike on any of these trails. It starts near Topton and winds its way up the ridge to Cheoah Bald. The last half-mile before the top is very steep and you may want to leave your bike at the bottom to save the push. Elevation at the top is 5,064 feet. The view is fantastic!

Start/Finish

From intersection of US 129 and US 19/74, drive north 2.6 miles on 129 and turn right onto the first paved road you come to. Drive up that road and park at the gate to Forest Service Road 259.

Trail Configuration

Out-and-Back

Surface

Single track • 2.2 miles
Gravel road • 12.8 miles

Highlights

Long uphill and downhill, superb panoramic views of Great Smoky Mountains National Park, Lake Fontana and Lake Santeetla

Total Distance

15 miles

Time Allowance

Beginner • 4 hours
Intermediate • 3 hours
Advanced • 2 hours

Mileposts

- From start, ride through gate and up Forest Service Road 259.
- Mile 6.3-- Bellcollar Gap.
- Mile 6.4-- gravel road ends at gate. Go through gate onto single track (old road).
- Mile 6.6-- road enters from right; continue straight on.
- Mile 6.9-- road forks; turn left up hill (the next half mile is very steep).
- Mile 7.5-- top of Cheoah Bald; turn around here.
- Mile 15-- finish.

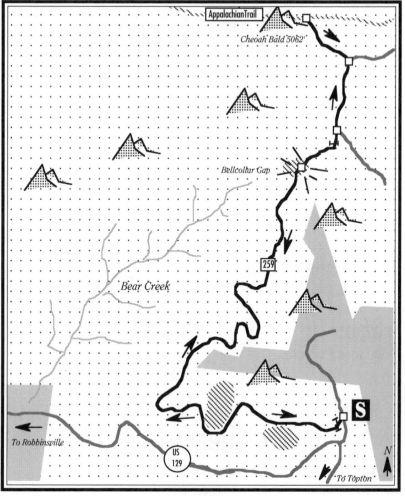

MAP KEY

Bike Trail........................	∿	Forest Service Rd. #.................	419
Other Trail or Road..........	∿	County Road Name.............	Watia Rd.
Direction of Travel...............	→	Foot Trail........................	∿∿∿∿
Start/Finish..........................	S	Timber Cut....................	▨
Milepost..................................	□		
Public Land.....................	[⋯]		
Private Land.....................	▬		
Railroad Tracks..............	┼┼┼		
Major Mountain..................	◣		
River, Lake, or Stream.....	∿		

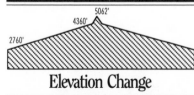

Elevation Change

2760' 4360' 5062'

19

Juts Gap

An easy, sloping, uphill climb. This road takes you up the ridgeline that lies between Robbinsville and Andrews.

Start/Finish

Gate to Forest Service Road 2616 (north 3.6 miles from US 19/74 on US 129)

Trail Configuration

Out-and-Back

Surface

Gravel road • 10 miles

Highlights

Loose gravel, views of Robbinsville and Andrews valleys, Bartram Trail crossing, long uphill and downhill

Total Distance

10 miles

Time Allowance

Beginner • 2 hours
Intermediate • 1.5 hours
Advanced • 1 hour

Mileposts

- From start, ride through gate to 2616 and up the hill.
- Mile 4.1-- seeded logging road turns off to right; stay left.
- Mile 5-- Juts Gap and Bartram Trail crossing. Beyond gate, road continues down other side of ridge but it has been seeded and makes for frustrating riding. It's best to turn around here.
- Mile 10-- finish.

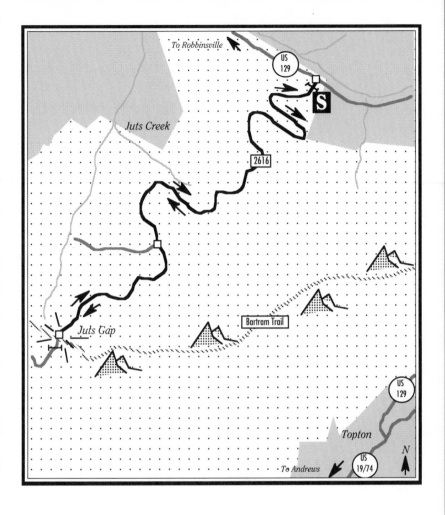

MAP KEY

Bike Trail............................	Forest Service Rd. #................. `419`
Other Trail or Road...........	County Road Name............. `Watia Rd.`
Direction of Travel............... →	Foot Trail......................... ~~~~~~~~
Start/Finish............................ **S**	Timber Cut......................
Milepost................................. □	
Public Land.......................	
Private Land......................	
Railroad Tracks............... ┼┼┼┼	
Major Mountain...................	
River, Lake, or Stream.....	

Elevation Change

3000'

1938'

PAVED ROADS

20– Burningtown • 18.7 Miles
21– The Road To Nowhere • 18.4 Miles
22– 711 • 25.1 Miles

Burningtown

Winding its way through the Burningtown Creek and Little Tennessee River valleys, this is a most relaxing ride. The route is entirely pavement with mostly moderately rolling hills. Traffic is light and you can get a true sense of life in the valleys of the Blue Ridge Mountains.

Start/Finish

Drive south from US 19/74 on Needmore Road to its end. Turn left onto Tellico Road and drive 3/10 mile to the first right turn, marked by a sign for Burningtown Church of God . Park on road shoulder and start here.

Trail Configuration

Loop

Surface

Pavement • 18.7 miles

Highlights

Old churches, river and streams, horse and cattle pastures, tobacco farms, views of surrounding peaks

Total Distance

18.7 miles

Time Allowance

Beginner • 3 hours
Intermediate • 2.5 hours
Advanced • 1.75 hours

Mileposts

- From start, take right fork and ride up Burningtown Creek Road.
- Mile 3.8-- paved road crosses creek to right; continue straight.
- Mile 7.3-- paved road turns off to right; continue straight.
- Mile 8.7-- turn left onto road just before crossing Iotla Creek (follow green sign for bike route 30).
- Mile 9.6-- turn left onto Rose Creek Road (follow green sign for bike route 35).
- Mile 14.9-- cross Little Tennessee River and turn left onto NC 28.
- Mile 17.8-- turn left and cross Little Tennessee River on Lost Bridge; bear right on other side down Tellico Road.
- Mile 18.7-- finish.

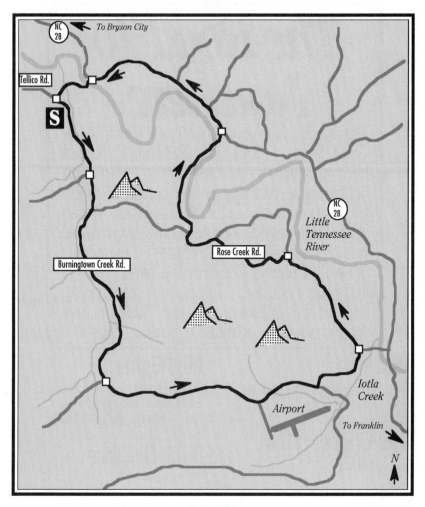

To Bryson City

NC 28

Tellico Rd.

S

Burningtown Creek Rd.

Rose Creek Rd.

NC 28

Little
Tennessee
River

Iotla
Creek

Airport

To Franklin

N

MAP KEY

Bike Trail............................		Forest Service Rd. #..................	419
Other Trail or Road...........		County Road Name.............	Watia Rd.
Direction of Travel..............	→	Foot Trail........................	
Start/Finish...........................	S	Timber Cut......................	
Milepost.................................	□		
Public Land........................			
Private Land......................			
Railroad Tracks..............			
Major Mountain.................		1938' 2200' 2120'	
River, Lake, or Stream.....			

Elevation Change

21

The Road To Nowhere

This route takes you from Bryson City into the Great Smoky Mountains National Park and back out again. In the early 1940's construction began on a road that would connect Bryson City with Fontana via the National Park. It was intended to provide a route to old gravesites and homesites swallowed by the park for the people of Swain County. Construction halted in 1943 and never resumed. This explains the sign you will see 2.6 miles into the ride: "Welcome to a road to nowhere....Broken Promise....1943- ?"

Start/Finish
Great Smoky Mountain Railway depot in Bryson City

Trail Configuration
Out-and-Back

Surface
Pavement • 18.4 miles

Highlights
All pavement, views of Smokies and Lake Fontana, tunnel, virtually no traffic, long hills

Total Distance
18.4 miles

Time Allowance
Beginner • 3 hours
Intermediate • 2.25 hours
Advanced • 1.5 hours

Mileposts
- From start, turn right onto Everett Street. As you leave town the road splits three ways; take the middle route straight ahead.
- Mile 2.6-- sign on left reads, "Welcome to a road to nowhere..."
- Mile 2.7-- enter Great Smoky Mountains National Park (gate).
- Mile 8.7-- gate across road; tunnel lies ahead 3/10 mile.
- MIle 9.2-- end of pavement; turn around here. *Riding on trails in the Great Smoky Mountains National Park is illegal.*
- Mile 18.4-- finish.

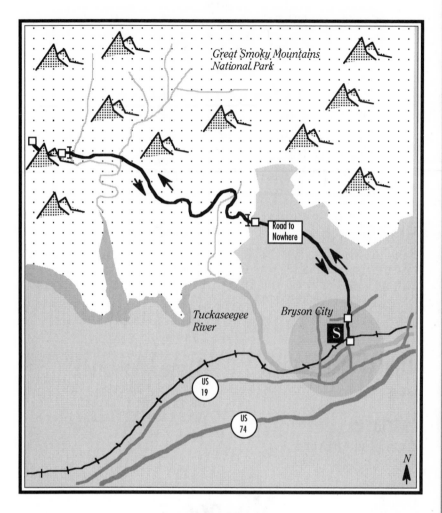

MAP KEY

Bike Trail............................
Other Trail or Road...........
Direction of Travel.............. →
Start/Finish............................ **S**
Milepost.................................. □
Public Land......................
Private Land.....................
Railroad Tracks.............. ┼┼┼┼
Major Mountain..................
River, Lake, or Stream.....

Forest Service Rd. #.................. 419
County Road Name............. Watia Rd.
Foot Trail.......................
Timber Cut.....................

Elevation Change

51

22

711

Except for the first half-mile, this ride is entirely on pavement. In places the surface is very bumpy with loose gravel, so take care on downhill turns. The loop winds its way along the side of Wayah Bald and then Lake Nantahala.

Start/Finish

From the Nantahala launch site, take the Upper Nantahala road to Burningtown Gap Road. There'll be a sign here for Forest Service Road 711. Start at the grass pull-off 1/2 mile down this road.

Trail Configuration

Loop

Surface

Gravel road • 0.5 miles
Pavement • 24.6 miles

Highlights

Great views, long uphills and downhills, Lake Nantahala, Bartram Trail, rough pavement

Total Distance

25.1 miles

Time Allowance

Beginner • 4 hours
Intermediate • 3 hours
Advanced • 2.25 hours

Mileposts

- From start, ride east toward Burningtown Gap on gravel road.
- Mile 0.4-- turn right onto 711, a paved road that climbs most of the next 12 miles.
- Mile 4.8-- first overlook.
- Mile 8.6-- second overlook.
- Mile 12.9-- Sawmill Gap, Bartram Trail crossing, and third overlook. Beginning of 10 miles of downhill.
- Mile 15.5-- turn right onto Upper Nantahala road.
- Mile 24.9-- turn right onto Burningtown Gap Road.
- Mile 25.1-- finish.

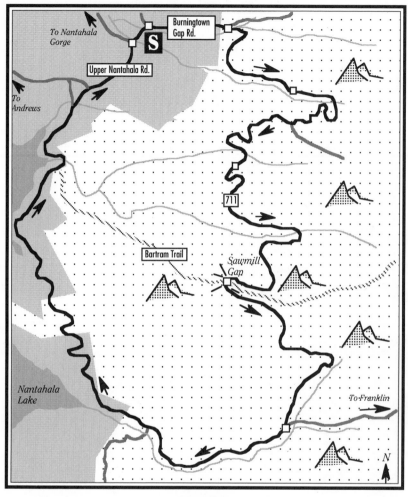

Burningtown Gap Rd.

To Nantahala Gorge

S

Upper Nantahala Rd.

To Andrews

711

Bartram Trail

Sawmill Gap

Nantahala Lake

To Franklin

N

MAP KEY

Bike Trail............................		Forest Service Rd. #..................	419
Other Trail or Road...........		County Road Name.............	Watia Rd.
Direction of Travel................	→	Foot Trail........................	
Start/Finish........................	**S**	Timber Cut.....................	
Milepost............................	□		
Public Land........................			
Private Land.....................			
Railroad Tracks..............	┼┼┼		
Major Mountain...................			
River, Lake, or Stream.....			

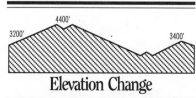

4400'

3200'   3400'

Elevation Change

TSALI MOUNTAIN BIKE TRAILS

Trail Information

In 1838, the U.S. Government ordered the Cherokee Indians to move from their home in the Blue Ridge Mountains to a reservation in Oklahoma. A sixty-year-old chief named Tsali and his followers refusing to go fled into the surrounding mountains. After ten years the government coaxed him into surrendering his life by promising his people land. It was on this land that the Cherokee Qualla Indian Reservation was established.

Just south of the reservation is the Tsali Recreation Area, managed by the U.S. Forest Service. For years, Tsali has been recognized by mountain bike enthusiasts as one of the best areas in the country for riding. With close to thirty miles of single track along the shores of Lake Fontana, it's no wonder.

Until recently, mountain biking at Tsali was on the shady side of legal. The trails were constructed many years ago by volunteer help from several local horseback riding associations and were therefore designated as horse trails. As the number of bikers using the area increased, the Forest Service decided to take a proactive approach. There are currently two complete loops at Tsali. The new loop, under construction and ninety percent complete, will be finished in the spring of 1992. The plan is to alternate use of the loops by horseback riders and bikers on a monthly basis. Check the information board at the trailhead before your ride.

The USFS is also pushing ahead with construction of two additional trails, totaling 10 miles. Completion of these is dependent on funding and volunteer help.

Tsali is a wonderful resource and an excellent example of how the mountain biking community can work together for trail designation.

Please be aware that small changes in the trails at Tsali are continually being made. The maps which follow are current as of this writing.

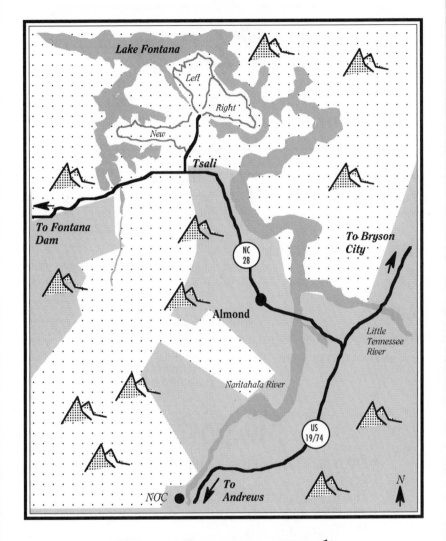

Directions to Tsali

From the junction of US Hwy 19/74 and NC 28, drive north on NC 28 for 3.6 miles. A U.S. Forest Service sign on the right marks the entrance to Tsali Recreation Area. Turn right here and drive down the gravel road 1.5 miles. At this point you have four choices. You can park at this junction to ride the new loop. A left turn will take you to the campground. A right turn will take you the the boat ramp. Driving straight ahead will take you to the trailhead for the left and right loops.

23

Left Loop

Highlighted by a view from a cliff high above Lake Fontana, this is the longest of all the Tsali rides.

Start/Finish

Tsali Recreation Area horse trail parking lot

Trail Configuration

Loop

Surface

Single track • 11.9 miles

Highlights

Single track, creek crossings, views of Smokies and of Lake Fontana, mud bogs, deadfalls

Total Distance

11.9 miles

Time Allowance

Beginner • 3 hours
Intermediate • 2.25 hours
Advanced • 1.25 hours

Mileposts

- From start, take left trail from parking lot (follow signs).
- Mile 6.2-- take left fork and follow blue blazes.
- Mile 6.3-- enter timber cut.
- Mile 6.5-- first mud bog.
- Mile 6.6-- second mud bog.
- Mile 7.5-- hidden trail on right is a short-cut to the junction of County Line Road and the right loop.
- Mile 7.7-- County Line Road enters from right. Continue straight on.
- Mile 8.2-- cliff overlooking Lake Fontana.
- Mile 9.3-- trails junction. Continue straight onto County Line Road.
- Mile 9.8-- turn left at clearing.
- Mile 10.5-- Meadow Branch Road enters from left. Continue straight on.
- Mile 11.9-- finish.

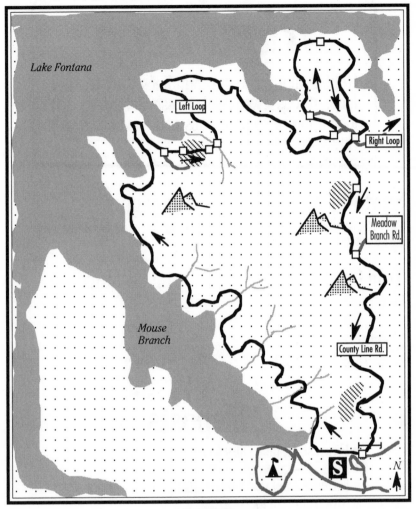

Lake Fontana

Left Loop

Right Loop

Meadow
Branch Rd.

Mouse
Branch

County Line Rd.

S

N

MAP KEY

Bike Trail............................	
Other Trail or Road...........	
Direction of Travel...............	→
Start/Finish.........................	**S**
Milepost.............................	□
Public Land........................	
Private Land.......................	
Railroad Tracks.................	+++
Major Mountain..................	
River, Lake, or Stream.....	

Forest Service Rd. #.................	419
County Road Name.............	Watia Rd.
Foot Trail.........................	
Timber Cut.......................	

1840'   2020'   2000'

Elevation Change

24

Right Loop

Rolling along the contour lines, this is a fast loop. It has fewer creek crossings than the left loop and not so many ups and downs. It's best ridden counterclockwise.

Start/Finish
Tsali Recreation Area horse trail parking lot

Trail Configuration
Loop

Surface
Single track • 11 miles

Highlights
Single track, creek crossings, views of Lake Fontana, deadfalls

Total Distance
11 miles

Time Allowance
Beginner • 2.75 hours
Intermediate • 1.75 hours
Advanced • 1 hour

Mileposts

- From start, take right loop (follow signs).
- Mile 2.8-- take right fork (watch for blue blazes). A left here will take you to County Line Road for a much shorter loop.
- Mile 5.7-- turn sharply to the left (follow signs). If you continue straight, the trail goes out onto a point above the lake and then loops back to this same milepost.
- Mile 6.8-- turn right. A left takes you up Meadow Branch Rd. to County Line Road for a shorter loop.
- Mile 7-- trail forks. Bear left.
- Mile 8.4-- four-way trail intersection; turn left onto County Line Road.
- Mile 8.9-- turn left at clearing.
- Mile 9.6-- Meadow Branch Road enters from left. Continue straight on.
- Mile 11-- finish.

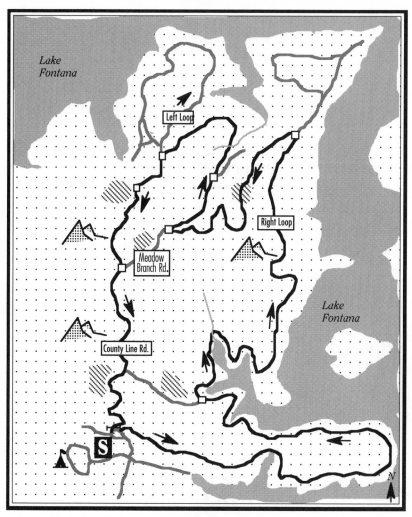

Lake
Fontana

Left Loop

Right Loop

Meadow
Branch Rd.

Lake
Fontana

County Line Rd.

S

N

MAP KEY

Bike Trail..........................	∿	Forest Service Rd. #.................	419
Other Trail or Road...........	∿	County Road Name.............	Watia Rd.
Direction of Travel...............	→	Foot Trail........................	〰〰〰
Start/Finish.............................	**S**	Timber Cut......................	▨
Milepost..................................	☐		
Public Land.......................	▦		
Private Land......................	▥		
Railroad Tracks...............	┼┼┼		
Major Mountain...................	⛰		
River, Lake, or Stream.....	∿		

1840'   2000'   2020'

Elevation Change

New Loop

This loop is easier and shorter than the other two. It has less grade and the one climb is gradual. A newly constructed trail, it will become smoother with more riding. Very few turns make this one easy to follow.

Start/Finish
Junction of Tsali roads

Trail Configuration
Loop

Surface
Single track • 6.6 miles
Gravel road • 1.4 miles

Highlights
Easy ride, loose gravel, creek crossings, Lake Fontana, views of Smokies, single track through rhododendron tunnels

Total Distance
8 miles

Time Allowance
Beginner • 2 hours
Intermediate • 1.25 hours
Advanced • 45 minutes

Mileposts

- From start, ride through gate and continue straight ahead.
- Mile 0.7-- clearing, trail forks three ways; take the far left trail.
- Mile 4.6-- timber cut; continue on trail.
- Mile 5.1-- fork at grassy area; stay right on main trail.
- Mile 6.1-- fork at grassy area; stay right on main trail.
- Mile 6.6-- trail T's into main Tsali road; turn left.
- Mile 8-- finish.

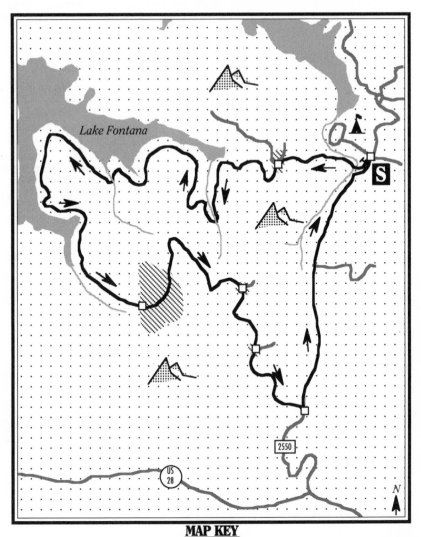

Lake Fontana

S

2550

US
28

N

MAP KEY

Bike Trail...........................

Other Trail or Road...........

Direction of Travel............... ➔

Start/Finish............................ **S**

Milepost.................................... □

Public Land........................

Private Land........................

Railroad Tracks............. ┼┼┼┼

Major Mountain..................

River, Lake, or Stream......

Forest Service Rd. #................. 419

County Road Name............. Watia Rd.

Foot Trail..........................

Timber Cut.....................

1760'   2040'

Elevation Change

Regional Information

The Area
Local Bike Resources
Riding On Forest Service Lands
Bike Etiquette
Lodging & Camping
Weather

The Area

Western North Carolina is a major vacation destination for millions of people each year. Many are drawn by the splendor of the Great Smoky Mountains National Park. What keeps them coming back year after year? That's easy. It's the beauty, the mild climate, the friendliness of the local people, the activities, and the attractions. Any time of year there are things to do and places to see. Whitewater rivers offer rafting, canoeing, and kayaking. There are lakes for swimming, fishing, and boating, and public lands for hiking, biking, hunting, and horseback riding. Cool mountain streams are perfect for tubing and trout fishing. Quiet mountain get-aways provide rest and relaxation. You can sightsee or recreate on foot, on horseback, by bicycle, automobile, or train. There is so much to do and see that even those of us who live here can't keep track of it all.

Local Bike Resources

- **Nantahala Outdoor Center Outfitters Store**
  41 Highway 19W
  Bryson City, NC 28713
  704/488-2175
  Bikes and bike accessories. Open year round, seven days a week. Located in the Nantahala Gorge.

- **Carolina Cycle Tours**
  41 Highway 19W
  Bryson City, NC 28713
  704/488-6737
  A division of Nantahala Outdoor Center. Offers guided bike tours. Located in the Nantahala Gorge.

Riding On Forest Service Lands

Biking in the Nantahala National Forest can be both delightful and confusing. Delightful because of the splendid infrequently traveled roads and trails that twist and turn throughout the Blue Ridge mountains. Confusing because of sometimes unclear rules and regulations. Almost anyone you talk to, inside or outside the National Forest, will give you a different interpretation of the regulations regarding riding mountain bikes. What trails are legal to ride? Which ones are not legal to ride? Until 1991, there were those who said it was illegal to ride on the trails at Tsali. Yet the trails were written up in two major magazines prior to that date and were at the time arguably the most popular riding trails in the Southeast. In this case, use certainly overruled any regulations. The issue always seems to fall into the grey area of governmental policy.

According to Dennis Coello in *The Complete Mountain Biker* (Lyons & Burford, 1989), "The use of ATBs is at present allowed on national forest roads and trails, except for those in wilderness areas or primitive areas, and on those trails marked with signs declaring **no bikes allowed** or declared off limits to bikes on the appropriate travel map." If this is true, as any avid biker hopes, any trail in the national forest, unless it lies within a designated wilderness area or is clearly marked "no mountain bikes" is fair game for riding.

In his 1991 report to the President entitled *Enjoy Outdoors America,* Secretary of the Interior Manuel Lujan, Jr. lists bicycling as one of eight major activities that can provide increased and diversified opportunities for safe and enjoyable outdoor recreation experiences on our public lands. The report's number one objective is to increase bicycling options through expansion, rehabilitation and construction of trails and to emphasize "multiple use trail systems (i.e., hikers, bikers, and horseback riders)."

Depending on interpretation, some of the trails listed in this book and many trails located on public lands could be determined illegal for mountain bikes. Experience leads us to believe that use is a major player in both future designation and current interpretation. In other words, a trail being used by a lot of mountain bikers is more likely to be considered okay to ride--Tsali, for example. Representatives of the Nantahala National Forest are very open to increased use of trails by bikers and would like to see use spread out throughout the forest, as opposed to the concentration of riding that is now seen on the Tsali trails.

The outlook for increased riding possibilities on public lands is getting better and better. The best way to contribute to this movement is to get involved by making the proper authorities aware of your wants and needs. Get to know the rangers and volunteer to help upgrade existing trails or build new ones. Most importantly, ride the trails as much as you can and encourage others to do so!

Bike Etiquette

The old phrase "use it or lose it" has never been more true than in the case of mountain biking on public and private lands. In this case it is even more appropriate to say "use it *properly* or lose it." It takes only a few incidents of irresponsible or abusive trail riding to close a trail, a recreation area, or an entire national forest to mountain bikers. There are numerous clubs and organizations that have developed a code of ethics for bikers. One of the largest biking organizations, NORBA (National Off Road Bicycle Association), publishes these guidelines:

- I will yield the right of way to other non-motorized recreationists. I realize that people judge all cyclists by my actions.
- I will slow down and use caution when approaching or overtaking another and will make my presence known well in advance.
- I will maintain control of my speed at all times and will approach turns in anticipation of someone around the bend.
- I will stay on designated trails to avoid trampling native vegetation and minimize potential erosion to trails by not using muddy trails or short-cutting switchbacks.
- I will not disturb wildlife or livestock.
- I will not litter. I will pack out what I pack in, and pack out more than my share whenever possible.
- I will respect public and private property, including trail use signs, no trespassing signs, and I will leave gates as I have found them.
- I will always be self-sufficient and my destination and travel speed will be determined by my ability, my equipment, the terrain, the present and potential weather conditions.
- I will not travel solo when bikepacking in remote areas. I will leave word of my destination and when I plan to return.
- I will observe the practice of minimum impact bicycling by "taking only pictures and memories and leaving only waffle prints."
- I will always wear a helmet whenever I ride.

You can interpret this code and others as you wish, but the major message to remember here is that you as an individual are part of a larger community and that your actions will be interpreted as representative of all mountain bikers. Responsible behavior goes along way toward creating a good image for everyone.

Lodging & Camping

- **Appletree Group Campground**
  Wayah Ranger District
  U.S. Forest Service
  8 Sloan Road
  Franklin, NC 28734
  (704)524-6441
  Forest Service operated, for groups of 10 or more only. Reservations required.

- **Freeman's Motel and Cabins**
  P.O. Box 100
  Almond, NC 28702
  704/488-2737
  Open year-round, cabins and rooms. Closest to Tsali. Reservations recommended in winter.

- **Nantahala Outdoor Center**
  41 Highway 19W
  Bryson City, NC 28713
  704/488-2175 or 800-232-7238
  Open year-round, limited hostel lodging available. Three restaurants (one open year-round, two open seasonally). Outfitter's store open year-round, seven days a week. Located in the Nantahala Gorge.

- **Nantahala Village**
  4 US Highway 19W
  Bryson City, NC 28713
  704/488-2826 or (outside NC) 800-438-1507
  Open March-December. Lodge, cabins, and restaurant--very good and reasonably priced. Located in the Nantahala Gorge.

- **Tsali Recreation Area Campground**
  Forest Service operated. Designated, very basic sites available on a first-come, first-served basis. No reservations, reasonable fee. Closed in winter.

- **Turkey Creek Campground**
  P.O. Box 93
  Almond, NC 28702
  704/488-8966
  Private campground. Close to Tsali and other rides. Open mid-March through late fall.

Weather

Month	Average Temperature*		Average Rainfall
	High	Low	(in inches)
January	47.5°	26°	3.48"
February	50.6°	27.6°	3.6"
March	58.4°	34.4°	5.13"
April	68.6°	42.7°	3.84"
May	75.6°	51°	4.19"
June	81.4°	58.2°	4.2"
July	84°	62.4°	4.43"
August	83.5°	61.6°	4.79"
September	77.9°	55.8°	3.96"
October	68.7°	43.3°	3.29"
November	58.6°	34.2°	3.29"
December	50.3°	28.2°	3.51"

*All temperatures are fahrenheit. Information provided by the National Weather Service.

Notes

Notes